Rocks and Minerals

David Lambert

Franklin Watts

London   New York   Toronto   Sydney

© 1986 Franklin Watts Ltd

First published in Great Britain
   1986 by
Frankin Watts Ltd
12a Golden Square
London W1

First published in the USA by
Franklin Watts Inc.
387 Park Avenue South
New York
N.Y. 10016

UK ISBN: 0 86313 359 2
US ISBN: 0-531-10165-7
Library of Congress Catalog Card
   Number: 85-51599

Photographs supplied by
Frank Lane Picture Library
M. Nimmo
M. Heyland
Steve McCutcheon
NASA
Novosti Picture Agency
Geological Museum, London
S. Jonasson
Dr J. Guest
US National Parks Service
David Jefferis

¾⅜Illustrations by
Michael Roffe
Hayward Art Group
Drawing Attention
Rob and Rhoda Burns

Designed and produced by
David Jefferis

Technical Consultant
Martyn J. Bramwell

Printed in Great Britain by
   Cambus Litho, East Kilbride

Rocks and Minerals

Contents

Inside the Earth

△ Quarries and gravel pits are good places to see some of the rocks beneath the soil. The pebbles in this gravel pit are bits of rock that have been broken up long ago.

If you could see inside the Earth, you would discover that it is made of different great layers.

At the center is an intensely hot, heavy core. Around this is a molten metal layer. Then comes the mantle, a thick layer of less dense rock. Some of this is so hot that it oozes about like sticky tar. The less dense rocks which make up the Earth's solid outer crust float on the mantle. These rocks lie below the soil and beneath the sea.

Just like a cake, any rock is made up of ingredients. We call these minerals. Most minerals are stony mixtures of pure substances called elements. More than 90 elements occur inside the Earth, but just eight form almost all the rocks of the crust. Indeed, three-quarters of the crust is oxygen and silicon. These elements form quartz, the chief mineral in sandstone rock and seashore sand.

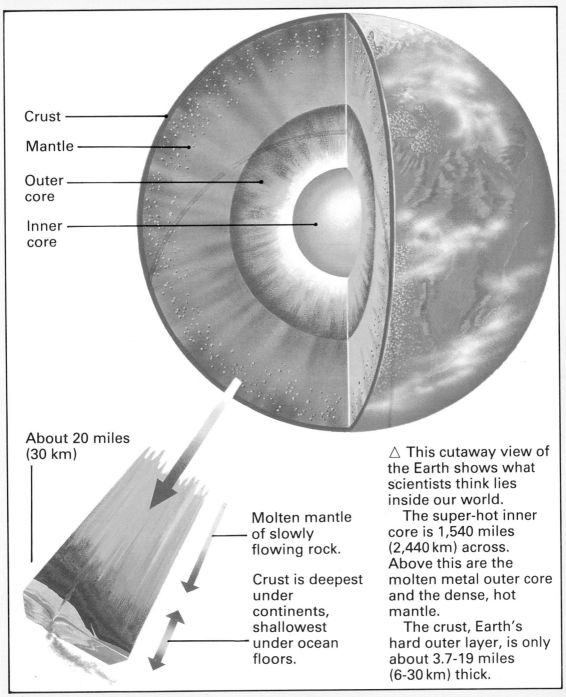

Crust

Mantle

Outer core

Inner core

About 20 miles (30 km)

Molten mantle of slowly flowing rock.

Crust is deepest under continents, shallowest under ocean floors.

△ This cutaway view of the Earth shows what scientists think lies inside our world.

The super-hot inner core is 1,540 miles (2,440 km) across. Above this are the molten metal outer core and the dense, hot mantle.

The crust, Earth's hard outer layer, is only about 3.7-19 miles (6-30 km) thick.

5

Recognizing minerals

△ Use an unglazed bathroom tile (the back of a glazed one will often do) to check a mineral's streak. Here, a small piece of pyrite leaves a black streak.

Various clues help you to tell one mineral from another. One clue is crystal shape. Most minerals are made of crystals with a special size and shape, although overcrowded crystals grow irregularly. Another clue is cleavage – the way that crystals break. A diamond splits in several directions, but a topaz splits in only one.

Hardness is a further guide. To find a mineral's hardness you try to scratch it with substances whose hardnesses are known. Experts using special instruments worked out that diamond, the hardest mineral, is four million times harder than talc, the softest.

Color varies with impurities in a mineral. But each kind of mineral tends to leave a tell-tale colored streak if you scratch it on a white substance harder than itself. Some minerals have a glassy, greasy or metallic luster. Mineral scientists (mineralogists) use these and other tests.

△ Haematite is iron-rich and gives rocks and soil a reddish color. Much of the world's iron comes from mines in the USA and Australia. Haematite produces a bright red streak and has a hardness of 5–6 on the Mohs scale.

▽ The hardness scale was devised by an Austrian, Friedrich Mohs, in 1822. The softest mineral is talc (1), the hardest, diamond (10). Each mineral in scale will scratch any mineral softer than itself.

△ Beryl measures 7½–8 on the Mohs scale. It often occurs in cavities in granite. This one is a green crystal formed in a chunk of calcite found in Colombia. Beryl comes in other colors, including blue, yellow and pink.

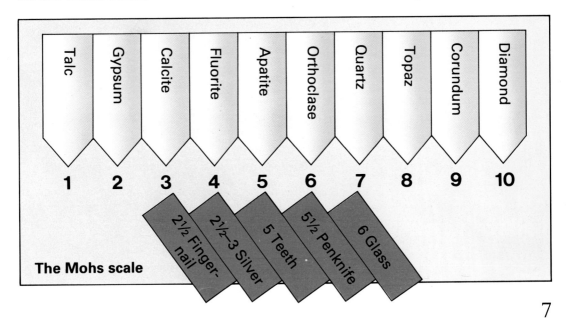

Talc	Gypsum	Calcite	Fluorite	Apatite	Orthoclase	Quartz	Topaz	Corundum	Diamond
1	2	3	4	5	6	7	8	9	10

2½ Finger-nail
2½–3 Silver
5 Teeth
5½ Penknife
6 Glass

The Mohs scale

How rocks are formed

There are three main kinds of rock, igneous, sedimentary and metamorphic.

Igneous rocks form from magma. This is underground molten rock that sometimes oozes up through the Earth's crust, then cools and hardens.

Sedimentary rocks are formed from broken bits of rock or from the remains of dead plants and animals. In time, all these bits and pieces accumu-

▽ This section through the Earth's crust shows where rock types may form. Movements in the crust may thrust some rocks high up as mountain ranges. Other rocks are forced far below the surface.

Sedimentary rocks forming from silt deposits

Fold mountains made of sedimentary rocks. They are thrust up by crust movements.

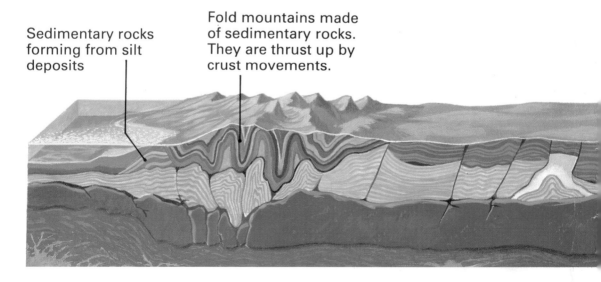

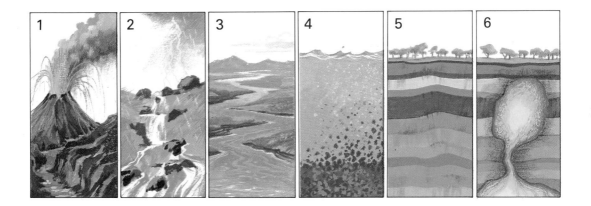

late as layers of mud, sand or shells. Then chemicals slowly change these layers to solid rock.

Metamorphic, or "changed" rocks can start off as either igneous or sedimentary rocks. They are changed by tremendous underground heat or pressure.

△ This diagram shows various stages in rock formation. **1** Magma forms igneous rock. **2** Weathering breaks down rock. **3** Rivers wash pieces to sea. **4** Particles pile up on sea bed. **5** These form sedimentary rock. **6** Heat and pressure can change igneous and sedimentary rock to metamorphic rock.

Metamorphic rocks created in new areas of volcano activity

Volcanic activity creates igneous rocks

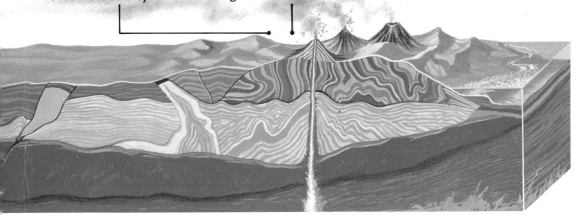

Igneous rocks

△ Molten lava spews from a volcano. Some of the world's igneous rock is lava that once flowed from cracks and holes in the ground.

Igneous or "fiery" rocks form as their molten minerals cool down enough to harden. Different minerals crystallize at different temperatures, producing different kinds of rock.

Some igneous rocks cool and harden slowly underground. We call these intrusive rocks because they have intruded, or pushed their way,

10

between the rocks already there. The minerals of slow-cooling intrusive rocks produce large crystals. You can see the crystals of feldspar, quartz, and mica in a lump of granite. This gray, white or pinkish rock is the most abundant rock of all.

Extrusive rocks are igneous rocks extruded, or squeezed out, from volcanoes. These rocks cool down too fast to form big crystals. The basalt that forms ocean floors is made of much finer grains than granite and obsidian is just a smooth volcanic glass.

▽ These granite outcrops are the remains of a vast blob of molten rock that cooled and hardened deep underground. Wind and weather have worn away the surrounding rock and soil, leaving the much harder granite exposed.

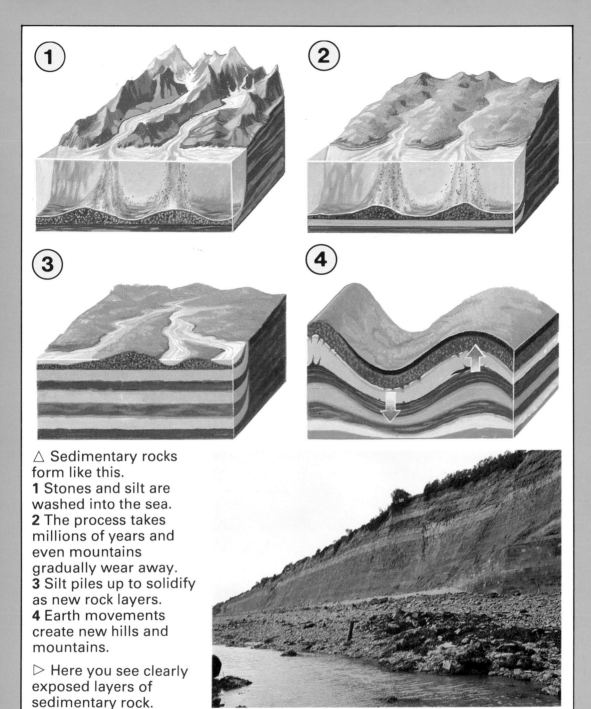

△ Sedimentary rocks form like this.
1 Stones and silt are washed into the sea.
2 The process takes millions of years and even mountains gradually wear away.
3 Silt piles up to solidify as new rock layers.
4 Earth movements create new hills and mountains.

▷ Here you see clearly exposed layers of sedimentary rock.

Layered rocks

Sedimentary rocks form where layered sediments are squashed together or are stuck by natural cements.

Rivers wash huge quantities of broken rock into the sea. On the seabed, silt slowly hardens into silt-stone, sand turns to sandstone and pebbles stick together to form con-glomerate.

Other layered rocks form where the hard remains of dead sea plants and animals pile up on the seabed. In places, billions of tiny shells make up limestone, full of fossils.

Yet other sedimentary rocks form as the Sun's heat evaporates warm, shallow pools of water, leaving behind the salts that they contained. These salts accumulate to form thick beds of gypsum and rock salt.

In time, the Earth's slowly moving crust may heave sedimentary rocks above the sea to form mountain ranges.

△ Chalk cliffs are the remains of billions of tiny creatures that died and sank to the seabed many millions of years ago.

Chalk is soft and easily crumbles away. Here, the cliffs have worn away, leaving chalk stacks, rising out of the water.

Caves

△ This cave system is typical of those found in limestone regions around the world. Caves are popular places for potholers to explore. The bigger cave systems are often open to the public. Special lighting reveals the beauty of the underground world.

△ This cave system is typical of those found in limestone regions around the world. Caves are popular places for potholers to explore. The bigger cave systems are often open to the public. Special lighting reveals the beauty of the underground world.

Streams and rivers slowly wear away rocks raised above the level of the sea. Running water carves valleys in the rock. Water also trickles down through crevices in limestone, dissolving calcium carbonate, the rock's main ingredient. So the crevices grow bigger until some form huge cave systems that stretch for long distances.

Inside caves, dissolved rock can reappear in strange new forms. This happens where water drips from a cave roof. Some water vanishes into the air as water vapor, but it leaves a thin, shiny layer of calcite sticking to the rock. It takes a hundred years to form a very thin layer of calcite.

In time, long calcite spikes called stalactites grow down from the cave roof and calcite spikes called stalagmites grow up from the floor. If they meet they form calcite columns that resemble organ pipes.

△ This photograph reveals the fairyland world inside a Spanish cavern. Gleaming stalactites and stalagmites spear toward eath other, jutting from roof and floor.

Changed rocks

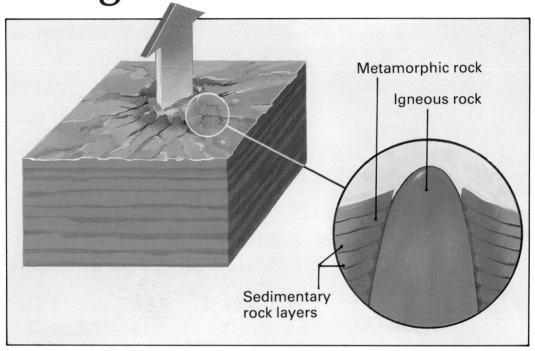

Metamorphic rock

Igneous rock

Sedimentary
rock layers

△ This diagram shows how metamorphic rock may be formed. Molten magma wells up through layers of sedimentary rock. The heat and pressure change the sedimentary layers to metamorphic rock. The magma cools and hardens to form igneous rock.

Great heat or pressure can make new minerals from old in several ways.

In places, blobs of molten magma push up through the Earth's crust, baking and squashing the solid rocks around them. This changes the soft rock clay to the much harder hornfels and turns limestone into marble, often seen when it has been polished.

Hot, rising gases may concentrate metals from igneous rocks. Dissolved

16

minerals trickle into crevices in rock, then harden into veins containing copper, gold or other metal ores.

Deep down in the crumpled mountain ranges, heat and pressure alter huge areas of rock. Here, mudstone can turn to slate. Added heat and pressure turns slate to mica-schist, a rock with shiny mica flakes. Even greater heat turns mica-schist into a banded rock called gneiss.

△ Mines such as this provide slate, a metamorphic rock produced from clay and shale. It splits easily along lines of weakness to provide flat sheets which can be cut to make roofing tiles.

17

Prospecting and mining

△ A prospector "pans" river gravel for gold. A few specks in the gravel may be flakes of gold. The flowing water can carry gold particles far from the solid rock in which the yellow metal formed.

Knives, cars and many other useful objects are made mainly of metals such as aluminum, iron and copper.

Finding the mineral ores was slow, hard work when mineral prospectors had to search by eye. Now instruments speed up the hunt.

Magnetometers show up magentic ores containing iron, and seismographs detect underground rock layers by the "echoes" they reflect back when seismologists set off explosions.

Miners tunnel deep down to follow narrow veins of ore. But strip mines are the largest and machines strip away the soil. Then huge power shovels scoop up vast quantities of iron, copper or aluminum ore from the surface.

Once miners have dug up an ore it goes to a refinery that separates the useful substance in the ore from waste substances that can be thrown away.

Seismic prospecting

Shock waves from small explosions bounce off various rock layers. The waves are picked up by geophones and recorded on a seismograph.

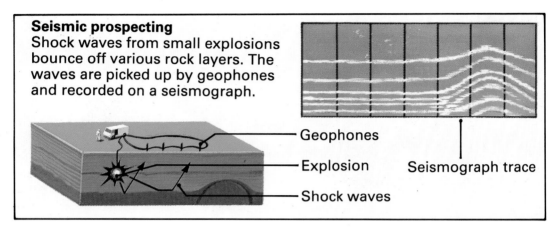

Geophones

Explosion

Shock waves

Seismograph trace

Magnetic prospecting

An instrument called a magnetometer is carried aboard a plane. It shows whether the flight passes over magnetic rocks which may include valuable ores.

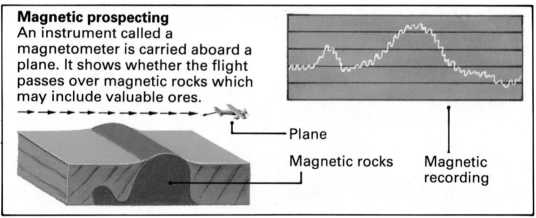

Plane

Magnetic rocks

Magnetic recording

◁ Mine works look very similar all over the world. Here you can see typical corrugated iron buildings and a covered belt for moving large amounts of rock and rubble.

19

Collecting specimens

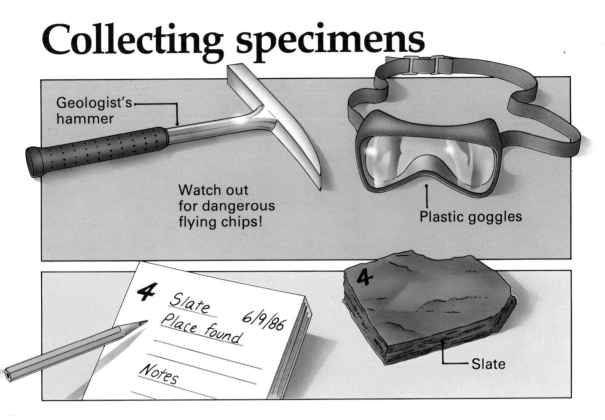

Geologist's hammer

Watch out for dangerous flying chips!

Plastic goggles

4 Slate 6/9/86
Place found
Notes

Slate

△ Here are three useful rock collecting items. The special geologist's hammer is designed to split rocks. The goggles are to protect eyes from flying stone chips. Marker pen and notepad let you make notes and label specimens.

Discovering beautiful or interesting rocks and minerals is fun. You need a hammer, goggles, magnifying glass, collecting bag, wrapping paper, notebook and marking pen or pencil.

Chip pieces from the rocks that show in cuttings, cliffs, quarries or on mountainsides. But keep clear of clifftops. Find examples of different kinds of crystals and choose pieces that will fit in a small box. Write down where

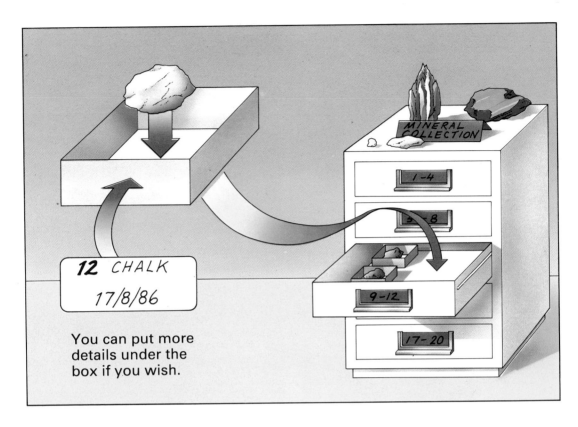

12 CHALK
17/8/86

You can put more
details under the
box if you wish.

you find each specimen.

At home you can clean and trim the specimens and then arrange and label them. Field guides and geological maps may help you identify some rocks and minerals, but you need expert help as well.

Study any minerals shown in you local museum and make friends with experienced collectors. You might also join a mineral society.

△ Here is one way to show and store a collection. Each piece fits in its own small box, numbered and labeled with the name, place where it was found and date of the find. Lots of boxes will fit in a small filing cabinet.

A mineral collection

You should be able to collect many of these minerals yourself. You could buy others in geological museums – they often have small specimens for sale at reasonable prices.

△ **Apatite** This rather soft, glassy mineral can be clear, white or pale brown, green, blue or yellow. It occurs in teeth and bones. It includes phosphates which are used as fertilizers for crops and plants.

△ **Calcite** Soft, pale glassy calcite crystals can form plates or needles. Calcite is the main ingredient of marble and limestone. A few microscopes have lenses made of clear calcite.

△ **Corundum** Its six-sided crystals are among the hardest of all minerals, at nine on the Mohs scale. Corundum is used in tools that grind or polish. Transparent forms include the red ruby and blue sapphire.

△ **Feldspar** This name describes an important group of minerals, a main ingredient of igneous rock. Feldspar contains aluminum and silicon. It is also used in making glass and porcelain.

△ **Galena** This is a heavy, soft, gray material. It provides our main supply of lead. The ore occurs in veins, with holes where cube-shaped crystals of galena grow. Some of the finest crystals come from the Midwest.

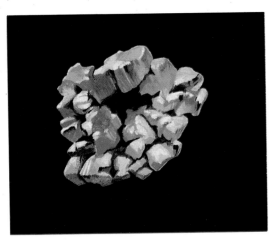

△ **Gold** Gold is a rare, soft yellow metal that never tarnishes. It forms as tiny particles in certain rocks, especially in South Africa. People have long valued it as money and for making jewelry.

△**Graphite** This black, greasy form of soft carbon is used in lubricants, paints and pencil lead. The world's main producers of graphite are China, USSR, Mexico, Korea and India.

△ **Gypsum** Soft, white gypsum crystals formed where old inland seas dried up. The ancient Greeks used the mineral to make plaster casts. Now gypsum is used in paints, paper, plaster and cement.

△ **Olivine** Olivines occur in the Earth's oldest rocks. The glassy, greenish minerals contain silicon and oxygen, combined with the metals magnesium and iron. A gem variety, is found in Burma and Brazil.

△ **Pyrite** Prospectors call this brassy, yellow mineral "fool's gold" as it has fooled many prospectors over the years. It may look like gold, but it contains only iron and sulfur.

Quartz A hard, glassy mineral. Stone Age hunters made knives of flint, a type of quartz. Other varieties form the gemstones cairngorm and amethyst. Quartz sand is used in glass, bricks and mortar.

△ **Silver** This precious metal occurs in rock as tangled silvery wires and in ores containing sulfur. Silver jewelry was worn 3,000 years ago. Now, silver is also used for photographic film and printed circuits.

Sphalerite The main ore of zinc, which contains much sulfur. Miners threw it away until the 1860s, when a process was devised to separate the zinc from the sulfur. Zinc is a good rust-proofer.

△ **Sulfur** Pure sulfur crops up in volcanic rocks as yellow crystals. It also occurs in some metal ores. Sulfur is used in gunpowder, tires, fertilizers, medicines pesticides and sulfuric acid.

Talc A fingernail easily scratches this white, soapy material. Sculptors carve with soapstone, a kind of talc. Many homes use talcum powder, which is pure talc, very finely ground.

Gemstones

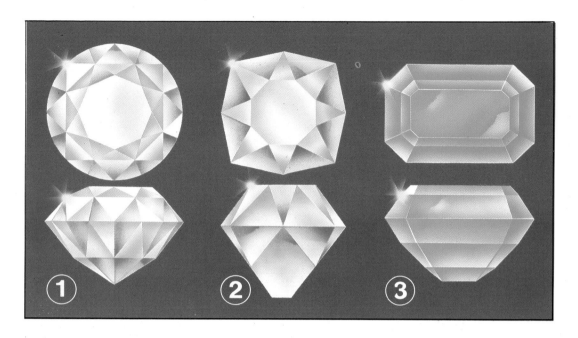

△ Here are gems cut in three ways, each with its own name.
1 Standard brilliant.
2 Square brilliant.
3 Step cut.
The flat surfaces of gems cut like these are known as facets.

Gemstones are minerals or stones used for jewelry because they can be cut and polished until they glow or sparkle. To cut a gem, an expert grinds away its surface with a hard abrasive; only diamond dust is hard enough to cut a diamond. Some gems are given rounded surfaces; transparent gems are made many-sided to reflect light.

Gems include such precious stones as diamonds, rubies, emeralds, and sapphires. Semi-precious stones include agate and amethyst. Many gemstones are simply rare forms of common substances. Rubies and sapphires are colored, transparent forms of corundum. Diamonds are just a pure, hard, form of carbon, the stuff that coal is made of. Yet a lump of coal costs very little while a fine diamond can be worth a fortune. How much a gem is worth depends upon such things as hardness, brilliance, color, size and rarity.

▽ This picture shows a geode of agate. A geode is a globular stone having a cavity lined with inward-growing crystals.

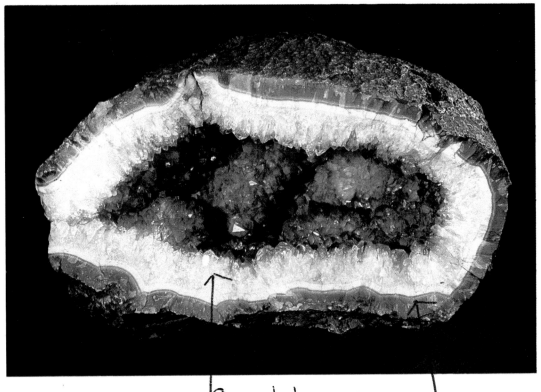

Crystals inside

Agate

27

Rocks from other worlds

△ Astronauts of the 1970s brought back many samples of moon rock for scientists back on Earth. This picture shows Harrison Schmitt, an astronaut on the Apollo 17 mission.

Astronauts or space probes have sampled the surface of several worlds, including the Moon, Mars and Venus.

We now know that the Moon's dark, dry "seas" are ancient flows of basalt, similar to those which form ocean floors on Earth. The hard, rocky crusts of planets such as Mars, Mercury and Venus are probably made of basalt too.

But the Moon's mountains are

mostly anorthosite, a rock found on Earth only in old parts of continents. The giant planet Jupiter has no solid surface – just swirling hydrogen gas.

Few minerals found on the Moon were new to science. One that *was* new is the mineral armalcolite. It was named after the American astronauts, *Arm*strong, *Al*drin and *Col*lins. Armalcolite contains iron, oxygen, magnesium and titanium.

△ Russian Venera probes took these photographs of the hot, rocky surface of Venus.

Glossary

Here are explanations of some of the technical words used in this book.

Core
The name for the center of the Earth.
It is made of molten iron with some nickel, sulphur and silica.

Crust
Outer layer of the Earth. Continental crust is made largely of granite. Oceanic crust is mostly basalt.

Crystal
A mineral which forms with regular flat surfaces, often transparent.

Element
Pure substance, not made of a mixture of various ingredients.

Igneous rock
Rock formed of magma that has cooled and hardened.

Luster
The soft reflective sheen of a mineral.

Magma
Molten rock deep within the Earth.

Mantle
The thick layer of dense, hot rock below the Earth's crust, above the core.

▽ Here you see rough opals and a piece cut to reveal its blue-fire beauty. This rounded cut is called cabochon.

Metamorphic rocks
Igneous or sedimentary
rocks changed by heat,
pressure or both.

Mineral
Ingredient of rock. Most
minerals are
combinations of two or
more elements.

Mohs scale
Scale for measuring
hardness, ranging from
soft talc to hard
diamond.

Ore
Any mineral deposit
that can be mined for
profit.

Rock
Solid substance made
up of a mixture of two
or more minerals.

Sedimentary rock
Hardened layers of
mud, sand, shells or
similar substances
usually deposited under
water.

Streak
The color of a
powdered mineral. It
can be tested by
scraping a sample
across a piece of
unglazed white tile, to
leave a colored tell-tale
mark.

Pronouncing the words

Agate
(*A-gate*)
Anorthosite
(*an-OR-tho-site*)
Apatite
(*A-pa-tite*)
Armalcolite
(*ar-MAL-ko-lite*)
Basalt
(*ba-SALT*)
Calcite
(*KAL-site*)
Calcium carbonate
(*kal-si-um KAR-bo-nate*)
Conglomerate
(*con-GLOM-er-ret*)
Corundum
(*cor-UN-dum*)
Feldspar
(*FELD-spar*)
Galena
(*gal-EE-na*)
Gneiss
(*nice*)
Gypsum
(*JIP-sum*)
Graphite
(*GRAF-ite*)
Haematite
(*HEE-ma-tite*)
Hornfels
(*HORN-felz*)
Igneous
(*IG-nee-us*)
Magnetite
(*MAG-ne-tite*)
Magnetometer
(*mag-ne-TOM-e-ter*)

Metamorphic
(*meta-MORF-ik*)
Mica
(*MY-kah*)
Mica-schist
(MY-kah-SHIST)
Mineralogist
(*min-er-AL-O-jist*)
Obsidian
(*ob-SID-ian*)
Olivine
(*OLLY-veen*)
Ore
(*OR*)
Phosphate
(*FOS-fate*)
Pyrite
(*PIE-rite*)
Quartz
(*KWOR-tz*)
Sapphire
(*SAF-ire*)
Sedimentary
(*sedi-MENT-ary*)
Seismograph
(*SIZE-mo-graf*)
Silicon
(*SILLY-con*)
Sphalerite
(*SFAL-er-rite*)
Stalactite
(*STAL-ak-tite*)
Stalagmite
(*STAL-ag-mite*)
Sulfur
(*SUL-fer*)
Talc
(*TAL-k*)

Index